BLUE ROSE

Poetry Novel

By: Kamaya Thompson

Copyright © 2009

Kamaya Thompson for McClure Publishing, Inc.

All rights reserved. Printed and bound in the United States of America. According to the 1976 United States Copyright Act, no part of this book may be reproduced or utilized in any form or by any means, electronic or mechanical, including photocopying, recording, or by any information storage or retrieval system, except by a reviewer who may quote brief passages in a review to be printed in a magazine or newspaper, without permission in writing from the Publisher: Inquiries should be addressed to McClure Publishing, Inc. Permissions Department, 9624 S. Cicero, #175, Oak Lawn, Illinois 60453. First Printing: July 7, 2009.

The author and publisher have made every effort to ensure the accuracy and completeness of information contained in this book, we assume no responsibility for errors, inaccuracies, omissions, or any inconsistency therein. Any slights of people, places, belief systems or organizations are unintentional. Any resemblance to anyone living, dead or somewhere in between is truly coincidental.

ISBN-13: 978-0-9790450-6-6
ISBN-10: 0-9790450-6-1
LCCN: 2009932581

To order additional copies, please contact:
McClure Publishing, Inc.
www.mcclurepublishing.com
800.659.4908
mcclurepublishing@msn.com

Acknowledgement

I would like to acknowledge Anthony Hollins. His caring spirit has taught me the importance of living each day as my last, and that each given day is another chance to do what I love - share my gifts with others.

Next, I acknowledge my grandmother, Iza Berry, a queen and strength of my family. Her love has covered me everyday of my life.

Lastly, I give respect to Gwendolyn A. Mitchell; an inspirational poet whom I have admired since I was a child. Her art has encouraged me to continue writing, and make my dream of published poetry into a reality.

Dedication

Blue Rose is dedicated to the memories of
Keldrick Kentrell Jackson
Nova Henry
Ava Curry
Three angels who lost their lives
to gun violence.

Blue Rose
Poetry Content

Table of Contents

Page

1. the say so 9
2. Perhaps made a Maybe I'm Unsure of 10
3. Cool 11
4. Aid 'Em 12
5. Action 14
6. Ms. Education 15
7. days 18
8. 44 18
9. Fear 20
10. and i never will 21
11. My Proverb 23
12. Juice 24
13. Ammunition 25
14. Outspoken 26
15. Never 27
16. If They Only Had a Brain 28
17. Me and Mr. Bubbles 28
18. Hair 31
19. ellipses disguised as a question mark 32
20. Saying I Love You 33
21. Bitter Sweet 34
22. Hero 35
23. Front'n 35
24. I'm Not Angry 36
25. Between Time 39

26. Over the Rainbow 39
27. Mystery 40
28. Home 42
29. Percussion 43
30. B4 I Breakdown 43
31. Zoe 45
32. Inspiration 47
33. Rain 48
34. Rise 'n' Shine 51
35. Blue Rose 52
36. Show Me God 54
37. on the flipside 55
38. can't get it out of my head 57
39. Homecoming 58
40. Adulessons 59
41. Cells 60
42. Memo to Self 61
43. Showtime 62
44. Read me 63
45. And Eat It Too 64
46. Searching for Self 66
47. Spirit of Dance 67
48. Sprout Wings 68
49. that's how it is 70
50. Star 71
51. Pretenders 72
52. Silent Revolution 73
53. Remedy 75
54. SOS 76
55. Then Now 77
56. tick tock 77
57. Trapped 78
58. Stand 80
59. the sky roars 80

60. Verb	81
61. the tongue	82
62. Dysfunction	83
63. title for my tears	85
64. i hate love	86
65. you are you are	87
66. i am F'n sexy	88
67. minutes	89
68. Weirdo	90
69. Ink	90
70. Motivation	91
71. can't say it enough	92
72. New Chapter	94
73. Trivial Love	94
74. I Don't Care	94
75. Anonymous	96
76. arms open	97
77. Divine Order	97
78. happy birthday!	98
79. home alone	98
80. if only	99
81. marionette	99
82. Premonition	100
83. what pain feels like	101
84. To You	102

Blue Rose ~ Poetry Novel
Xamaya Thompson

the say so

>Some people call it talent. Some folks say it's a gift. Some say it's a passion. Others may consider it a hobby. But, I and only I, truly know the correct term for it.
>
>The scientific probable cause for this overwhelming urge to retrieve a writing utensil may simply be reduced to a nervous syndrome of some sort....
>
>That sophisticated bullshit is inaccurate. Only I can state what this term is. I call it:
>
>*love. spirit. soul. my womb and casket. life. freedom. air. me.*
>
>I write. No. I don't actually. I...share.
>
>I share myself with the world, and all those willing to listen. I share my love, spirit, soul, and I will do it forever.
>
>It cannot be determined in one lifetime, how much I share and how much you grasp from it. But, dammit, as long as this pen sits between my thumb and index finger; you can bet your last dollar that you will be pleased.

Perhaps made a Maybe I'm Unsure of

the dreamers dream
the builders build,
I am them
so what's to come
of my creation?
I put it on and
took it off
like it's some kind of
fashion statement.
My insecurities hinder
me from making the
indentation I want
to make in your life,
so I sit alone
and ponder why
I'm here and why
the future is detached
from what I want to have.
Where I want to be
is something like the
Land of Far Far Away.
A place,
nowhere exactly,
more like a state
of mind.
She invited me in and
I accepted the invitation,
but the party was not as
live as I anticipated.
Now I blame myself for
not becoming the life;
for not bringing out the
animal in me

to pump the hype.
Regret is
a bitch that swallows.
What's to come
of my life?

Cool

       I put my head down.
       I don't care anymore.
       This crappy maze they call life is
       unbearable to endure.
       I just let go,
       by allowing thee to breathe.
       I take a break, I relax, I say at ease.

       'Cause I'm done, yea man, I'm through.
       I kick my feet up,
       and focus on the blue.
       'Cause my cloudy days are surrounding me,
       and while there's a little bit of light,
       I'm going to enjoy it for its time.

       'Cause it's coming, I said, I see it coming.
       Hell is on its way.
       But, before it arrives,
       I'm a live the good life.
       Time's running out.
       I'm losing the reason to have
       something to smile about.
       I need to find something to live for
       before I die;
       so I'm living
       for what I'm willing to die for….

I'd die for this pen
I know I'd die for the stage
Yea man, I'd die for the film
That's right, I'd die for the page.

So, I live for this pen
I said, I live for the stage
I just live for the film
I live for the page.

And before I let it go to waste.
I chill.
I put my head down,
I dream for one last time.
Before I get stressed out,
I live for what I'd die.
And that's cool.

Aid 'Em

The cops tell us to go home as we stand ready for the revolution, screaming, *Hell no! We won't go!* The officers are on the rebound. All we want is peace now. The streets are on fire. Handcuffed and on your knees. Please, stay together until we get a peace treaty. United we kneel. Tell me can you feel the media vesseling us through the tube? The whole world is watching, but it's not the channel you tuned in to. We are kids birthed by change. The black pants, blue collar, hard helmet, nightstick is ready to erase our name but we protect the same.

We seek a new world,

one accepting of girl on girl, guy on guy. Middle finger in the air, unzip your fly. A world eliminated of poverty. Where every citizen can afford property and the pensions never get suspended from the economy. A world where the war is no more, because violence is omitted from the vocabulary. Where education is not an opportunity but a standard, and every race in the White House is demanded. No fences on the border, no terrorist attacks. No knowledge of the term red neck, chink, or wetback, because every individual is equal as a man.

So we stand on the shore of Lady Liberty holding her torch and reject the patriots wishing to have the Children of the Revolution aborted. We protest in the name of the red, white, and blue.

The whole world is watching

for a change in these you-knighted-statistics-of-a-mere-I-can-not-stand-it! Reputations get abandoned when every child and man get together to fight a common cause. Watch the world get involved and allies form to revolutionize

the kingdom come. Our day has come.
Sam Cooke's change will come.

Turn your tv off.

Action

I have the power to be
who I want to be.
I am the creator of my
future
present
and my
past.
I hold the key
to my identity.
I am the me
I want to see.
No one but I
can define myself.
I am my better
and my best.
Today I take control
of my actions
by controlling
my thoughts.
I am my own boss.
This is my time.
lights camera action
Watch me shine.

~ Blue Rose ~
Poetry Novel

Ms. Education

They be acting like picking up a book is against mankind. Knowledge is like food, and believe, I gets mine!

The uneducated proceed to chase dreams, and unfortunately, half the world's been catching Zs. I guess the teachers have been getting paid to not do their job. My buddy didn't graduate, not because he had straight A's, but because he was tardy too many days. Yet everyday he showed up, just not on time; same as his graduation, one year behind.

Somebody please help them get it! Education is not an obligation, it's a privilege. Do you know how many people intentionally let their heart stop so you could be better off? And the same amount of people that don't want you to!

"See ya later mom!"
"Ok, have a good day, son!"
Soon as the car pulls off and turns around the corner, You're scooped up in your boys Monte Carlo. And for what! To go have a good time planning a future that reads: *No Life*.

Well, it's Wednesday and Mickey Ds got that 39¢ special, and I got 3 bucks to spend on anything I want, so instead of having school lunch, I think I'll like …go there. So my parents can think I'm in class planning a future to enroll into Hampton, when really my ACT scores will get me … nowhere.

Kamaya Thompson

Oh yeah. It's like that. Besides, my English teacher is
wack! I've been to her after school, three times, and
each time, we argue over each assignment; she just
don't like me!

Or it might be….

That she's tired of seeing you after school, instead of
in class, while you're hanging with your boo
who treats you like Boo Boo the Fool, because he
ain't in college and you ain't in school!

Wake up!

Wake up and see! Scholarships come from more than
football and cheerleading. They'll deny you from a
resume' but you'll always be drafted if there's
something in your brain.

And you say: "School ain't for me."

Our ancestors stayed up all night with flashlights
trying to read, and over a century later you'd rather
spend the day sleeping!

*Don't take it personal but, it's just me! I'm mediocre.
No, we can't be together! I'm not ready for a college
relationship. Masters Degree, we're just two different
people. I'm here, you're there, and there's nothing
…right…in here.*

*I'm with GED now, and we're happy together!
No, I didn't have an affair with Associates, it's too
much work! Ph.D.! Stop, you know I can't be
challenged! I'd rather work for McDonald's, we get*

along well! The stained clothes, impatient customers, stress galore... and it offers great benefits! If I become manager, I get to wear a polo!
No more, average button ups for me! Sometimes I think about going back to school, but....
An education isn't my thing!
I can't look smart. I can't be challenged. I can't fill my mind with new ideas to revolutionize this nation and possibly change the world! Noooooooo!
That's not black! Do I look white or Chinese to you? No, I'm stereotyped as an ignorant, number one consumer, who can't pay my own bills or raise a family, and I want to live up to it! My history teacher taught me about white folks and a whole bunch of wars, so how do I know any different?

Tell your ancestors that. See how they'll react.
Is that going to be your excuse why you failed?
Because of the teacher, or because you didn't care about school! And when corporate America, or America, to be exact, asks you why you failed, are you going to blame them? Who will take the blame for our people?
We will!
Not our laziness
Not our poverty
Not our welfare
Not our mediocrity
Not even ourselves!

We will blame Ms. Education,
what a terrible teacher she was.

days

>time is precious and evaluates you at all cost.
do your best before time is lost. you may
think you know, but time is the boss.
when it's all said and done, just
be who you are. every
lesson learned is
learned through
time. please
give me
more of
mine.

44

Pride is not good
enough a word to
express how I feel
when I sit and realize
Yes we can!
We've come far by faith,
I'm certain MLK is
smiling in his grave.
Sojourner Truth,
Rosa Parks,
Harold Washington,
Oh my God!
All my people,
people of the world,
all my children,
little boys
and little girls.
From Moses

to Malcolm X;
we stand and declare,
November 4, 2008,
Yes we did!
The Middle Passage
has led a path to your feet,
as your Inauguration Day
is a dream inside of me.
The corpses that lie in the
seas rise from the waves as
tears pour down my cheeks.
The nooses that swung
from the trees are now
your hands waving
to the people.
We walked,
backs turned to the
Door of No Return
into a blind future
with a weak soul
forced to carry on.
I now know it was not
in vain, because of the
thousands of voices
shouting your name.
Sam Cooke knew
a change would come.
I believe this is the dream
King spoke of.
From the chains,
from the ship,
from the field,
from the fountains
of Jim Crow.
From the noose,

from the boycotts,
from the extinguisher hose,
from the marches and the riots,
from city hall,
to the White House.
I know this is not the end.
Thank you for a
Change I can believe in.

Fear

I wrote you a love song.
I want you to hear it
but I'm afraid
to sing it to you.
What if you don't like it?
Suppose you think it cliché
What if you think it's corny?
You're a beautiful girl,
I'm sure
you get love songs
all the time.
You may find
no interest in mine.
I can't do it,
it's too risky.
I may blow it for myself.
You may never
speak to me again.
You may think
I'm a creepy man.
I won't go through with it,
it's just a disaster
waiting to explode.

This is a song
you will never know.

He's so sweet.
He's so kind.
I'm tired of these
jerk kind of guys.
I believe
he's mister right.
If only I had some kind of sign.

and i never will

i said i wouldn't get anything on my shirt today.
dag! a tear drop stain.
i can't keep a promise, not even to myself
life breaks promises, and it does it well
my road took me to a place i didn't want to be,
pushed me through the door, locked it, and threw
away the key
that force was impossible to bear
painful memories ringing in my head
and there i stood watching.

no pleasant movie
no pepsi and popcorn

just tears being forced not to shed
just smiles aching to spread
just the smell of death
all running through my head
and running did not become of me
no, i couldn't move my feet

Kamaya Thompson

life's experiences never fade
no matter how much longer after
the date has taken place
memory truly is a shame

tears screams
faces hugs
dance song
limo roses
stones suits
black white
hands hat
camera pulpit
mic nods
silence casket
hate

mama said there's no such word as hate
but mama this time you're wrong

i hated it all!

i hate that feeling of alone
i hate the hole
the empty, only can cry about it, hide your face,
i can't take it anymore,
Hole.
that memory i've tried to bury
but because i know where it's hidden
it can't escape from me.

when the trigger is pulled
the tears will fall
and down i will come
spirit and all

there is nothing that can describe
the true essence of a
pain and loneliness blend,
i can't get over it...

My Proverb

What's the point of living life
to follow everyone else's rules?
If we're living to die, why walk
a path that society chooses? I
hate life at times and don't
understand why, if I'm free, my
own tears I have to hide. I'm
trapped in my own house. They
want me to grow but won't
let me out, and if I leave early
I'm considered a problem child.

A lie and freedom, I can't tell
the difference. Used as an
analogy would make it a
complicated sentence. The
mind is powerful, can build
and destroy. But once unlike
the rest, it's retarded and
ignored.

Damage to others leads to
replicated pain. Damage to
self is mentally insane, or
is it product of not wanting
damage to others to replicate?

They say ask questions to
receive answers, but some
ask questions only to hear
what they want; and feel
insecure when it's not the
intended response.

Some live to die, others die
to live. I live for death because
heaven seems to be my only
residence. Me is all I can be.

Sugar
Honey
Iced
Tea

Juice

sounds like a screech
and I like it
pen
pad
hello, writer.
I like this.
like a fruit fly
on a fruit salad
I be on my notebook
'cause it's so good.

gimme dat flavor
it's major
the amount of ink

I pour out on this
paper
it's gracious
so amazing
can't wait to
publish this
creative work.
it's what I was
put on this earth for.
if the scientist could run a test
I bet their hypothesis
would be correct
because the guess is
that I'm the best
all the results say:
Oh Yes!
capable of conquering
anything you throw at me
call me the
manuscript athlete
you can't catch me
I'm unstoppable
all the proof is probable
no exact reason:
just because…
it's love!

Ammunition

and we fight
and we kill
until there's
nothing left
but blood

and we fight
and forget
what we were
fighting for
no mercy is
given in the
hands of
false love
this earth
will forever
be at war

Outspoken

And I vowed to never
sugarcoat shit,
even if it meant
losing love
at its own expense.
So quick to take
the defense, not
thinking about the
consequences I'd
have to live with.
I said I'd do less
talking and more
listening but
I didn't keep my will.
A loose tongue,
a looser mind.
I'm learning –
I'll get the full
lesson in due time.
I want to forgive

so first I'll start
with myself.
I confess,
my tongue and
I need help.
I'm sending out
an S.O.S.

Never

It's a lie. That word.

Happy.

There isn't such a thing.
I hate all those that say they have it.
It's impossible to be,
at least completely,

Happy.

Fucking sick joke
What a sick joke
Just a sick joke

That damn word.

Happy. Happiness.
Ain't happening!

No one can feel it.
None can be it.
Zilch hold it.
Few keep it.

I've experienced it,
but only until it fades.
That word is a game,
it visits then goes away.
The joy of life exists,
it's true,
it's always there.
But happiness is one
to share. And better to spare.
No one will have happiness,
the word itself is selfish.
Only liars claim to have it all
and it drives them mad.
Complete happiness
makes one sad.

If They Only Had a Brain

pe
opl
e
com
pl
ica
te
things

Me and Mr. Bubbles

i can't sleep
tonight because I'm
afraid of my
dreams. and

though I'm awake,
nightmares
are all I see.

on my back,
pillow flat,
darkness
surrounds me
I am trapped,
covers close,
there's no way
out. eyes open
or shut
the images haunt
me. I'm stuck.

death is like a
splinter.
grief is the pain
that stings
the nerves.
whether the
woodchip is
in or being
pulled out it still
hurts.

the comfort of
others is gone.
I am alone.
cheeks wet,
sheets are cold,
arm extended, for
it's you I hold;
my head on

your nose.
there is no life in me
you, likewise.
all we share are two
brown eyes.
the lonelier I grow
the closer you become.
my arms fold.
your arms
remain numb.
fur warms my cheek,
the nightmares hide.
I dare not dream
because their
safe spot is behind my eyelids.

fear freezes
but never goes away.
the chill of
death blows
on my face.
palms sweat
on your furry tummy.
my bear hug
would suffocate
you if you had
breath.
the light
of day is hours
away. between the
hours you keep
me safe.

i close my eyes,
each time defeated....

sleep is a stranger
in this town.
when daylight
comes, my eyes
will never thank me.
but I thank you for
surviving the
night.

Hair

Don't care,
it's everywhere,
sexy as hell
in my eyes.
All over the place,
can hardly see,
need a headband to mildly tame.
Look in the mirror,
I say, *Aight!*
Turning corners
turned heads,
oohs and ahhs,
stares of all kind.
Brown with a hint of black,
curly,
thick,
far from flat.
My love is above me,
but still attached.
Today I refuse to wear a hat.
Up and down stairs,
in and out of doors,
wind blows you in all directions.

I lust my reflection.
Power held up by my neck,
a lightning that keeps me warm.
Beautiful you are,
to me you belong.
But, with every smile
there is a frown.
Young cashier tried to bring us down.
Girl, let me give you a flat iron.
No, thanks, I say.
You look wild, honey child,
You must be cray-zay.
You won't get a man that way.
I smile inside.
She must not know,
I'm gay.

ellipses disguised as a question mark

it haunts my sleep
it travels through time
it picks at me
it invades my mind
it's the saddest dream
while one still has opened eyes
it's a sleepwalking trance that won't say goodbye.

and I am lost
under the covers
the pillow begins to smother
my voice becomes smuggled,
if only the world had ears.
so I begin to struggle
someone give this demon a muzzle

because its snickers are all I hear
I am walking on needles and pins.

I ask this question,
I ask a millionandone times
I fear the answer of all things
in the world to be afraid of,
and the answer is yet to come;
this question intoxicates my mind:
What value will my life have when I die?

Saying I Love You

The tongue is the power of man.
For some reason, I don't understand
why I keep holding it as if it's gripped in my hand.
I want to speak, but there's so much I fear.
I need to let go, but the doing of it, I fail to adhere.
My mind allows the future to appear,
but reality may switch gears.
I want to talk.

I want to express.
But every time I'm ready, set….I second guess.
As a result, I regret. Got to shake this off my chest.
Just spit it out. I won't know the answer until the statement is sprouted.
Got to stop being doubtful, baffled, or afraid.
Gotta just say it. Just gotta say it.
After all, they may want to hear it.

Bitter Sweet

She could laugh! Oh, she could laugh!

Her insides could be falling out, heart split in two, half past bankruptcy, and holding an eviction notice, but I bet you wouldn't know it.

I call her, *the actress*.

Never won an Academy Award, Tony, Emmy, or Golden Globe; but don't get it twisted – she does deserve it. I call her: *the ultimate faker, Ms. Camouflage, one in disguise* – and trust me, you'd never know. She could perform joy in the midst of sorrow, sadness in a world of happy, black in sheer yellow, and make red look like pink – and I guarantee you wouldn't blink. You can call it a *façade, phony, fake, or say, "Damn, she's good!"* – but no one ever gets it. She does not have to pretend. On the sly she can be your friend, and she sho' can dance with her enemies.

It's so wonderful to watch her put on a show, but no one ever follows her home. When you're gone, the show is over. Ooh, wee! Isn't it sweet to watch her act, but for her it's just a knick knack, because no one knows that when she is alone the greatest show is put on!

Ooh wee! Isn't it sweet? To laugh, laugh! Cry, cry.

~ Blue Rose ~
Poetry Novel

Hero

I watch as the golden beauty dances in her throat.
A sight I could never turn my head from. I want to
hear another note. She recites the poetic black and
white I possess in my palms. She claims she doesn't
know the words, but every melody flows right along.
A silhouette of white and gray, a masterpiece in my
eyes. Together, we have found our passions, and
when she expresses hers, the pleasure is all mine.

A room for hundreds becomes a room for two as the
lake sits beyond the window view. She dances in her
notes and my eyes water. Only a heavenly father
could create a picture so marvelous. Promise me this
day will reside. I'm assured it will by the star in her
eyes. Her hair, her smile, her spirit, her voice; I'm
thankful for this joy.

I'm often puzzled, but today all pieces are attached. I
have begun a relationship until the day of the casket.
The poet and the gift of song. No need to wonder, my
doubt has been cured. I am loved by the singer in this
room. The golden beauty is my best friend. My heart
beats to your voice. Please sing again.

Front'n

if time grants me another day
I promise on that day
I'll hug you tighter than
the day before.
I tried to hide
my emotions by

possessing composure
and acting a role
unlike myself.
However, when you're
away I'm overwhelmed
with regret. Like damn,
I should of....

No more of that.
Time granted is
meant for taking
chances and I will
no longer delay.
You must know
my true colors, for
you put yours on
display.

I swear,
I put it to
rest. I will
love you to
death with
each and
every
second.

I'm Not Angry

Somebody kill me please!
Somebody kill me please!
Put a bullet in my head!!!
That's how I feel,
how I feel right now.

~ Blue Rose ~
Poetry Novel

If there's any better quote, it would cause for a competition.
I want to stop, drop, and roll out this earth
(with high honors)!
Don't cry for me please,
you don't really wanna!
I'm expressing myself,
don't look at me funny!
What, you don't understand?
Let me break it down for you!

Things That Piss Me Off:
- too much homework
- a packed schedule 8 days a week
- annoying little kids
- stupid teachers
- 6 hours of sleep
- super slow buses
- not being able to drive a car
- heavy book bags
- weather in Chicago
- an empty wallet
- low salary (yet I'm grateful I have some kind of work)
- how my religion urges me not to ball a fist and punch
- people telling me I'm doing too much

Too much?
Well, maybe I should add another pet peeve:
- telling me things I know already!

I have to get this off my chest, hey, I have to breathe!
And believe me,

I speak for more than myself
this is for my teens and all my adults.

<u>Things That May Piss You Off:</u>
- a bored boss
- uncontrollable road rage
- red lights
- daylight savings time
- stupid offspring
- the temporarily out of cash voiceover that continually repeats itself every time you open your wallet
- the fact that 10 more minutes turns into 20 after the alarm goes off
- knowing that you agree with everything I'm saying!

You are not alone!
So, what's next on this paper?
Let me tell you,
it gets better:

These Facts Won't Change For A While!

I'm content with these
annoying little figures that dance
around my brain on a daily basis;
they help me further
agree with what the first line has stated!
But no,
I'm not angry
let's just say,
I'm just sayin'!

Between Time

Boredom is a K-9 with a vagina.
Take the metaphor at your own risk.
I sit and wish
time could have sympathy
but at the rate of this tick,
I doubt the clock has any mercy on me.
Could it be
that I'm impatient and
have no respect for time?
Whatever be the case,
I'm going out of my mind.
I need freedom,
for this chair and clock
keep me confined.
Release me,
because patience' virtue
is not mine.

Over the Rainbow

      Where do you start when you can't finish a sentence? Mind constantly churning, brain twitching for a chance to hold on to what's missing. Odd kid out. Fighting for identity with what's underneath her blouse.
      Battling hetero v. rainbow; sexuality and spirituality never came so close, and I just want to come out. World leaders

don't do wrong. But who can define wrongdoing when we're all sinners and religions are composed of more than one – yet we say we all believe in God. What's right? What's wicked? Someone please give me a definition because as it stands, I'm one liberal ass Christian.

    I just want to be accepted, permitted, understood, respected; not rejected, discriminated, forbidden, or hated. Who will accept the kid that's labeled homo? I don't want to be labeled no more. I'm human, isn't that enough to be proud of? Will they still love me? Or will they never know? I just want to get over the rainbow.

Mystery

why do you
talk to me like
this?

why do
you push me
around with
your tongue?

physical contact
has not been
made, but you
do me harm.

I do not

like your
actions,
they are
unreal.

why do you
bring me
down?

do you
want to see
me fall?

you try to
act innocent
but your
intentions
are no
accident
at all.

you bestow
fault. I do
not like what
I see, why
does it
reside?

your intentions
are cruel,
there is no
truth behind
your eyes.

Home

black girl
she called me
black girl

I feel so
connected and
can't imagine
not being able to
express it
this is a life
learned lesson
this journey is
a blessing

a people united
are a people divided

but despite it
we walk with
heads held high
and eyes open
we were chosen
and I know it

black girl
she called me
black girl
and she's
black woman

I promise to
never run
from it

I am a black girl
and I love it

Percussion

>Nothing can kill you if you don't let it. The mind is the weakest link, making it a strength is what keeps it functioning. When the mind would rather give up, the heart presses on. Knowing which organ to follow is the malfunction this body stands on. Which is right? Which is wrong? There is a line between strong and weak. The body cannot function without a heartbeat. Though the mind is one of its own, there is something stronger that sets it apart. Every choice made follows the beat of our heart.

B4 I Breakdown

If I write another lyric,
if I sing another song,
would it keep me from
being alone?
My broken spirit weighs
heavily on my dome.
I've been holding back
tears, but I can't hold
any longer. Can't believe
my eyes can produce
so much liquid. Folks keep

asking what's wrong....
truth is, I need a
shoulder to lean on.
I can't keep feeling
like this.
They say death
is something that must
happen.
I can't keep living
with fears. I'm scared
I might be next, next,
next in the coffin.

If I write another poem,
add another verse, throw
another chord on the
keyboard, would it be
enough to surrender
my pain?

Gosh dang, I can't
keep hearing his
name. Life feels
like a runaway train
that won't hit the brakes
and I'm too afraid to
jump off the tracks
so I'd rather just stay.
Don't ask me.
Don't make me bleed.
Don't puncture the
hole where darkness
seeps. Don't look,
don't try to analyze
what's behind these

brown eyes. It's too
complex, too
complicated. I'm
too disturbed to be
investigated, don't
interrogate me.
Because I'm half a
centimeter away from
breaking down. I'm
losing my soul and
the grave is calling out.

If I write another word,
If I pick up this pen
one more time, will
it be enough to save
a dying soul
like mine?

Zoe

She came to get away.

A smile hiding pain. She arrived in the weirdest way, yet a way so common; so familiar, so cliché, that it caught me off guard. A greeting that we receive so often, we forget its significance. A salutation, an invitation into our lives, yet we do it so often we forget how much it's worth until it's deprived.

Young. No older than five.

She paid me a visit. She entered into my world the simplest way known to us.

Hug.

She hugged me. No question, no remorse, she took my waist by force. Weighed half of me, but somehow picked me up. The audacity to love a stranger. With her hand around my hips she looked into my eyes and spoke without motioning her lips.

She thanked me.

I could hear it. I could hear her spirit loud and clear and it begged me to embrace her back. How could I not react? I did what I'm so used to – I wrapped her small body, half my height, my hands on her shoulder.

We hugged.

Awkward. Weird. Who are you? Why? I'm….

How dare I!

The gesture of a hug is much more than bodies touching. It's people loving. Strangers or acquaintances saying welcome to my life. And she said it quite well. She reminded me the importance of hugging, and how often we forget. In fact, the embrace of a loved one is what we miss…and intensely, what we regret.

On this day, this child didn't give me a hug; she desperately took one.

A little girl alone at home as mommy talks business on the phone. A neglectful father, always on the road; only to be dropped off at grandma's who's trying to stay young and the last thing she wants to do is repeat playing mom.

She ran to me for a last embrace, because her fate was slipping away and the only love she had left sat around my waist.

Why?

Was it my face? Was it my smile? What did she see in me that made her run and hold me with such power? This girl. That girl. You. Maybe I needed the hug too. I may never know the reason why, but if ever she's having a bad day; if ever she begins to cry. She knows she can hug the girl with the bowtie.

Inspiration

there's something missing.
can't pen point it,
but I can feel it.
I need to be challenged.
give me something to do.
work me,
make me feel useful.
when there's silence,
put on music.
when it's cold,
let there be snow.
when there's an idea,
let it grow.

if it's so,
tell me why.
if it's gifted,
don't let it die.
if it attempts,
let it try.
if it is,
don't let it change.

you're seated.
get up or be ignored.
because life is
meant for movement,
it can't be sat through.
I'd rather run
than walk,
talk than be silent.
I ask questions
to have answers
provided. I'm alive
give me an activity.
because the last
thing I have
time for, is
sleep.

Rain

My insides are barely alive
and honestly
it wouldn't hurt if I died.
I'm hungry,
but not any meal can suffice.
I am hungry for life

in a world of smiling faces,
friendships,
wide open spaces…

I don't want to be a burden
so I'd rather not say shit.
Silently I sit and ponder
how to change this
fucked up situation.

For a week
the weatherman said
it's going to rain
and I don't want to rain
on the parade.
Funny,
I wonder why
it didn't rain today.

A physical
and mental
contradiction.
I and the weatherman
are liars
beyond description.
My smile is false,
only my tears are real.
And no matter how
I feel, I can not heal.
So I fear.
I fear losing a bf
and most of all I
fear losing self,
so I just smile and wave
because no cloud

should be in the sky
on this sunny day.

The forecast said
showers upon showers
on this day.
I just can't allow
myself to rain
on their parade.
Why didn't it rain today?

As great of a day
as it was, it
rained anyhow.
The rain
on the inside of me
couldn't help from
leaking out.
The sun, the heat,
the white clouds
all turned gray.

It rained
it stormed
and it's all
my fault.
I guess the
weatherman
was right
after all.

Rise 'n' Shine

Can't sleep tonight.
My dreams are keeping me awake:

places I want to go
experiences I want to touch
people I want to meet

I dream with my eyes open

goals I want to reach
hands I want to shake
conversations I want to have

Can't sleep on my dreams

I sit on this beige carpet
back to the bed
no pillow for my head
I can't get comfortable right here

Dream-catchers don't sit…we swing

constantly moving to a silent beat
a rhythm of thought
mind forever churning
throat burning to speak
eager to learn from the teacher
even if the teacher is life itself

I'm always prepared

ready for the world
starting a new edition

focused on the future
and all that's offered in it

I'm flying and I can't land
waiting for reality to birth from my head

Goodbye
Good Night
Good Morning

Blue Rose

    She sits. Delicate. Patient. Modest. The definition of beauty. In a room of colorful wonder, she sticks out as obvious as can be. A flower of indigo leaves. I refuse to leave the store without her hugging my sleeve.

    In awe, amazement, awesome attraction, and awestruck ambience, she is absolutely not artificial. A character of her kind blows my mind, for I never imagined a day in my life I would fall in love with a flower, but it has happened. She is symbolic and has now become apart of me. Blue is all I see.

    So often does mankind go out of its way to purchase red, white, or pink; but I have spotted blue. Similar to the others, she bares leaves and a green stem, but it is what's inside of her that sets her apart. She is dark. Her melanin reveals through her leaves, making her arms a beautiful blue-green that puts my spirit at ease. Her texture is smooth and fair, my God, she is rare – and that rarity forces her to not be taken for granted. She stands tall, sprouting each day, and I observe, awestruck and amazed. Before my eyes, natural beauty takes place.

Yes, she is still a rose, but I know she is so much more. She represents the life of all. The delicacy that in time will fall, but as it stands, it chooses to stand tall. No, she can not be seen everyday, and I'm sure she will one day wither away. But before that stage takes place, I vow to honor her beauty while it is unchanged.

Some things in life are so common we tend to overlook, but when it is gone we long for chances we wish we would've took. A blue rose comes along and it is a far cry from being red.

I will distinguish my reds from blues. A red rose may come and go, but the blue rose deserves a second glance. There is a blue rose in my best friend. A blue rose in the woman from whose womb I began. A blue rose in the life I live. A blue rose in this pen. Don't overlook the blue rose. Never take it for granted, always remember it will one day wither, leaving only its memories to share.

If ever you get the chance, and I'm sure you will; be sure to pick the blue rose in the field.

Show Me God

your words
your tears
your testimonies
all serve
a purpose,
right?
answer me;
Why
am I alive?
How
did we get here?
Who
created mankind?
show me.
prove
Adam was
the first man.
convince me
to understand.
Why
should I
believe in
higher power?
Why
should I
believe at all?
nature
is not enough.
the galaxies
persuade me not.
I will not
praise what I
cannot see.

you have to
try harder
to make
me believe.

on the flipside

Taking a little breather can't possibly hurt. That's what I said before I never awoke. The world expects me to do my work, but I need some new teachers! They stacked me up! They nearly broke my back! My shoulders were aching before I was able to put on the second strap! But hey, I won't complain. After all, I got two weeks for winter break!

That's more than enough time to get these studies out the way. In fact, today, I'm going to clean my slate. I'm typing on my HP, with a healthy meal to eat, Doritos and meat to be precise you see! I'm Googling, and even playing my jam. But right now…I'm tired.

Let's see…hmmm…

I'll turn on the TV, no harm in that! It's midday, I can have another snack. My dog is bored; I'll go for a walk. My phone hasn't been ringing, I think I'll dial and talk. I'm on the web already, I can Google that some other time. MySpace, Facebook, You Tube, Yahoo Messenger, might have a line.

I'm not procrastinating….no!
I'm just…let's see……hmmm…

…I'm just occupying my mind!

There's no need to get all skeptical and technical, I'll get my work out the way. I'm just taking five for about five days. Hey, I got two weeks! Gheez! Don't get all sophisticated with me.

It's called *homework*. I'm at *home,* and I'm *working*!

It's just not work from school. I mean, it's not like I'm ignoring the fact that I have to do it! Whoever said it was a crime to listen to music? When was it ever unhealthy to play a strategic game? I want to beat the high score, isn't that stimulating the brain?

What do you mean, *procrastinating!!*

I'm just….chuuh…
I'm juuust….
lemme lemme seee…

I'm just being patient about how I want to organize my academic activities. Yeah, that's it! So don't you go getting all skeptical and technical, because it will get done!

Huh!
Why didn't I do what?
School starts tomorrow!
Well see what had happened was…
I…um…well…lemme seee….
…uhh…help me
….how could I put this

….uhhhmmm….
chuuuuuhhhhh………
……I don't know?

can't get it out of my head

cheer up, kid
trouble don't last always.
that's hard to believe
when pain's engraved
in your brain.
seems strange
to release memories
from your noggin
but it's all too simple
for the same to
cause blockage.
it's awful,
too awful to think.
I'm caught up,
but I can't release.
The situation is
just as serious
and it keeps me
just as furious
and it still is
just as hideous
and the feeling is
just as painful
since day one
'cause I can't
get it out
of my head.
and it's been

just as painful
since day one.

Homecoming

I run to you like a mother who hasn't seen her child in a million days. I fiend for you like freedom to a slave. When I'm away from you, life goes upside down. I need you. You're my source of power. I left you for some time and my mind went out of business. I'm scared, frigid, lost, and alone. I'm half of half of whole. I'm the answer to no. I'm not a product, yet alone a person. I'm a mistake. A wrong turn. A failure and a captive. A tear drop - when I'm away from you.

I'm a one-man football team, and I'll always lose the game. My cheerleaders have turned away and fans have moved to the other side of the stadium. Everything's gone wrong. Why did I leave you for so long? You're my cure, and I stopped taking my medication. Forgive me, I need a replacement. I'm dying and I can't stop. Give me your hand, lift me up.

These expectations on my back are beginning to ache, and lately I've been dropping the weight. I've got to pick it back up, or I'll surely lose the game. Here I am, take all of me; flaws and all. This is me. I can't pretend to be perfect any longer.

My spirit is dying and so is my flesh. Before I drift away, please let me express my love for you. Let me apologize. I left you alone, turned my back and walked away. I have returned prepared to say, I'm in need of serious help. I'm in distraught, distress, damage, and I need to become undone.

With all pride aside, I ask this once:

teach me
teach me again
remind me how to love the pen,
my closest friend

Adulessons

I'm sixteen, and in two months I'll be seventeen, so in one year I'll be eighteen; which technically makes me an adult, you see!

But no matter the mathematics, a sixteen year old child holds no adult status. Adulthood is what I'm planning, but on this planet, it seems like grown and kid have no average.

Every kid's dream is to be grown, and all the old people want to be young. Yet where the crossroad lies is a mystery to all.

When will it happen? I want it to come about! I dream of the day I'll be out my momma's house. When I can run away and be running to myself; when I can pay bills like everybody else.

I want to be grown!
An adult!

Living the life of choices and no rules! I want to get in my car and ride to the destination I choose, and never hear of a curfew.

I want to be free!
I want to know what it's like!

Who put the slow motion on my teenage time? Dude, let's get it crackin'! I want to walk into the room and see what's happenin'! I want to be able to stop a youngster from *my* adult conversation!

16, 17, 18….and life!

One more year, two months, and the world is mine! I want to move fast and listen slow! I want to be able to make my choice! I know responsibility runs up and down and through life no matter your age, but dang, when I'm grown,
responsibility is mine to take, not an obligation.

I want to live life to and fro
I want
to be a kid no more

Cells

I share the soul of Jonathan Larson
the same poetic views of Langston Hughes
named after Maya Angelou
inspired by Lady Sings the Blues
my spirit rises to notes of Mary J. Blige's voice
I rock out to Panic! At the Disco
and embrace the techno vibrations of Metro Station

I am Phillis Wheatley fused with Jill Scott
I am Fall Out Boy with a little bit of Common
Alicia Keys plays her piano inside of me
with a dash of Sammy D.
I am a gift sitting on the porch of Avenue Q
as Alice Walker picks me up for a Spike Lee Joint
debut

Stevie Wonder, Yellow Card,
Erykah Badu, Coldplay, and Cobra Starship
India Arie sings to this Aries
and through these inspirations I breathe

West to Hova
Morrison to McMillan
Giovanni to Perry
Winfrey to Taylor
through my fingertips these inspirations exist
through my voice they are heard
you are the reason I proceed
thank you for allowing me to be

Memo to Self

Some heart it must be to keep me inhaling and
exhaling day to day, because today it would be best if
I didn't anymore.

My memory is picturing images I've tried for months
to ignore, but my brain refuses to adhere to my heart,
and I can't stop whether my eyes are open or shut.
It's torture, trust me.

It's the way the body works. You tell yourself that one way or another you'll get over it, but somehow you prove yourself wrong. I don't know where I belong, but I do know I'm not alone; and I don't like where we are.

Move me. Move me to a place where I can forget. Where the eyes are dry, and the pillows, shirts, and sleeves aren't wet, and the nose doesn't need tons of tissue towelette, and the mouth doesn't moan, and the teeth don't grit.

I need closure, composure, or at least, a shoulder. Because right now, I can't depend on myself. Why? Why? Why? No! How,
did I get into this mess? I don't care anymore; just get me out of it! Keep me away from myself, because my eyes have seen too much and my mind likes to recycle. Please, somebody, take away this reminder. I don't want to remember anymore.

Showtime

Hey there!
Hey you, with the bowed head!
Get up and prepare for the challenge!

You have not been given the spirit of fear
so smile and believe you can.

You're capable of making the big win
so get with it!
Do your thang and make us proud!
Suck it up and

hold your head high.
The day is anticipating triumph,
just believe and all is yours.

The world is depending on your success
so don't you dare consider
yourself second best!
Prepare, be proud, and be the proof.
It's time to shine
the spotlight's on you!

Read me

If I screamed, would the paper shout back?
If I bleed, would the ink turn red?
If I cry, would this paper be wet?
When I die, would you have wept?
To see,
I put this stick that drools ink
between my fingers and scream!

I scream
throw chairs
pull out major strands of hair
throw an old lady down the stairs
and simultaneously
put my middle finger in the air.
I release emotions that reveal
no composure,
but on the outside
I look still,
frozen.

I'm silent if you refer to my lips,

but if you refer to my grip
you'll know that silence
does not exist.
With this utensil I roar,
I bitchslap teachers and mothers
with no remorse.
With this pen I burn frequency
through my throat, and no joke,
I am a murderer
a killer
massacre initiator
victimizer
kidnapper
Nightmare on fucking Elm Street!!
But if you look at me,
I'm just jeans and a tee,
innocent, sweet.
You never would've known.
Come inside my dome.
Read me,
if only for a moment.

And Eat It Too

This woman occupies my
mind and I have reason to
believe I recycle her thoughts
just as well. My game has
been knocked off its
wheels ever since my
pupils laid sight of her
features; I haven't been
able to shut my lids.
Some female she is.

~ Blue Rose ~
Poetry Novel

I swear I've never
felt like this. Some days
I can't control my senses
and on others, I've
composure that keeps me
frozen as her beauty
possesses my limbs.
I am weak in her presence.
So weak, I obtain a strength
I never knew I occupied.
A passion deep in my
bloodstream. This lady
drives me wild. She is
fragile, delicate, and I
respect her with all I am.
I'm in love with this
beautiful creation,
needless to say. And I
have loved her since
my eyes took its first
glance. She disagrees,
but she is the perfect
woman. I do not doubt
that her feelings for me
are mutual; yet we do not
share these thoughts.
Instead, we frolic around
one another like two lovers
with a slice of cake – no
one wants to take the last
piece. So we just dance
around the issue politely.
Suppose I am growing
mature with time. I am
hungry, dammit, I'll take

the slice; and I will offer
to share if I feel so obliged.
I will not let the sweet treat
of love go to waste. Let's make
haste. Our first kiss awaits.

Searching for Self

fighting for survival is a task alone.
waiting for tomorrow is a burden that burns.
doubt is a fear that yearns to escape,
yet there is no key to this gate.
life is a maze of choices
and voices unlike my own. I'm
trying to find my tone.
Listen.
open your ears and close your eyes.
reach with your mind. I need to
find my own voice again, and
everything will be alright. I
want to listen to I.
then will I know which path is right.
I don't know where life will
take me next, but on this
quest let me find self with no regrets.
let me decide what's right for I.
but it can only be done when
my heart agrees with my mind.
I listen for my voice,
but first,
let there be silence.

Spirit of Dance
dedicated to Anthony Hollins

I'll dance for you, even when the music stops playing.

I'll write for you, even when the ink runs dry.
I'll stand for you, even when my calves start aching.
I'll speak for you, even when the world stops listening.

Whatever it takes to keep the dream alive,
all the hope that's needed to feel a sense of pride.
In a world that will turn its head from the truth,
or close its ears to the loudest cry;
I'll dance for you and keep your heartbeat entwined with mine.

With my feet, I'll lead a path to success.
With my hips, I'll sway to the beat of freedom.
With my arms, I'll release all doubt into the sky.
With my eyes, I'll look up and see you smiling down.
With this body, I'll step until I soar.

I'll dance for you until my soul can dance no more.
With my movement, the world will see and understand - nothing can stop the spirit I have within.

I'll dance, and with my dance I'll speak.
I'll dance, just as you have taught me.

Sprout Wings

I feel like….

falling
failing
standing
straight up
ignoring
trying
never
give up
running
drowning
catching
reaching
out my palm
crying
striving
screaming
I don't give a #@*!

I want to….

listen
keep wishing
shooting
for my
ambitions
I'm distant
and cringing
but I want the
attention
keep hoping
keep going

pursuing
each goal
without
regretting
notion
I keep this...

pen between my limbs
without losing
train of thought
This world is....

provoking
lonely
at times
I don't know
where I'm
going

If there's a....

chance
I'll grab it
I want to
hold on to
my last
because if
I let go too soon
the answer
won't be
unmasked

There's only....

one route

no room
for doubt
if I want
to catch
my dreams
I've got to
grab wings
and sprout

that's how it is

tryna be cool
breakin' all the rules
growing up fast
parents just don't understand

that's how it is!

lyrics run sprints
rockin' fly kicks
cashin' checks so paper's in my pocket

that's how it is!

holla just because
never fall in love
gotta keep up
gettin' what cha want

that's how it is!

learn to play the game
loser ain't my name
life is a stage

it'll never change
we like it that way

that's how it is!

Star

If you asked me why I live,
I'd tell you for my dream.
If you asked me again,
I'd tell you the same thing.

Your expectations do not define me,
so I have no reason to plead.
I am myself,
and I have no intentions in changing.
I was put on this earth for the purpose that I believe.
The only fact that we have in common
is our option to breathe,
so please, don't interrupt me.
Don't interrupt my goal.
Do not disturb my integrity.
Don't cut off my pride.
Don't turn your head from my beam,
because I am shining!

I am glowing,
sprouting rays of radiant beams
and you can't help but see.
I am shining,
and I do it naturally!
I am a wonder for all to take sight!
I am me, and I am bright!

My life is like a star,
the biggest one there is.
Just because you don't see,
doesn't mean I have disappeared.
I am me, I am bright,
and I live off my dream.
Yes, my dream enlightens me!
So please, go ahead, be on your merry way.
But know, wherever you are,
you will get a glimpse of me!

If you asked me why I dream,
if you asked me once or twice,
I'd say;
to light up your life!

Pretenders

I wear the mask that foolishly hides
and repeatedly asks the question:
Who am I?

I wear the mask that is ashamed
and confusingly titled: *No Name*

I wear the mask embarrassed to be,
that cannot smile, ashamed of its teeth.

A mask with no eyes, yet is not blind,
but somehow sees everyone but itself.
It's like a shell, unable to escape. It's
illiterate because it does not turn the page.

It is abandoned and holds no knapsack.

And worst of all – it's black.

I wear the smile of the mask, because
it is not my own. Behind the mask, the
smile is gone. Insecurities eat me alive.

You see me. You say you see. You see?
You say you see me, but you're wrong.
You see the mask I put on.

I wear the mask that wants to love, but
gives no embrace when we hug. I am the
mask I wear and it's not for decoration.
My mask brings me humiliation. I want
to take the mask off, but my face is not any more
appealing.

You may think you know those you
look in the eye, but you'll be surprised
the deception behind it. You do not have
to wonder any longer; the mask you view
is one you wear too.

I can admit. I have been falsely accused,
because everyday I am not what you view.
It's painful enough to think that I have been
lying to you about my identity. But trust, the
pain gets worse, because I lie to myself
in the mirror.

Silent Revolution

A dream is a noun,
yet it can also be a verb.

Kamaya Thompson

A dream is invisible,
if it can not be heard.
You can do for yourself
better than others can do for you.
But what's the purpose,
if others can't share in your joy too!

we all want
we all need
we all wish
we all dream

But how will this be accomplished
if we do not speak?
You can fight for your right,
you can die for your dream,
you can debate your opinion,
but will you grab a sword for your voice?

The mightiest man
conquered not by himself,
but with the majority beside him,
therefore he had to speak.
It's complicated to understand a deaf teacher.
So why become deaf yourself?
The definition of a leader,
is to be unlike everyone else.
How can you have your own note
singing the same song?
Start a new beat,
and the band will play along.
You can't know what's right,
if you never do wrong,
so step outside the box,
to create your own.

A change will come
once you make one,
and that change can be the way of life!
You can be anything you want,
if you first strive!
Freedom lies inside the mind.
There is no such thing as a silent revolution.
In order to be,
you must make them hear you.

Remedy

I need it.
I'm begging
for it now. I've
got to have my ink.
Like an alcoholic
for a drink,
give it to me!
When the pain is
too much to bear
I run to my pen.
It soothes my soul.
This utensil helps my
emotions flow. This
here is more than a
poem. It's my comfort.
The world is harmful
and full of wicked smiles.
When I'm lonely I pick
up the pen and dial.

I call to a distant place.

A place that removes
heartache, write away.
There's nothing better
to find sanctity in -
a pen in hand, my
medication.

SOS

Can I talk to you?
I'm having trouble hearing myself.
It's becoming hard to do what's best
for my reflection and I'm becoming
infected with this ball of confusion.
I've been told a thousand times before
the difference between right and
wrong but now I'm starting to forget.
Can you help refresh my memory?
Consequences don't make sense
until they're in action; I'm
trying to prevent them from
happening. I want to win.
Can you help me win this fight?
I'm at war with myself and the
blows are mighty. It's in me,
the potential to call a truce, and
right now the score is at deuce.
Can you help me decide?
I can't choose for myself.
I want to do what's right but
my opponent thinks differently.
Please.
Can you help me get out of my own way?
For I can't push my weight;

if I lose this round,
I lose my faith.
There's only one thing I request.
One thing I need:
Help me not be my worst enemy.

Then Now

My mind wanders for peace in this wild world
that hosts hearts so fragile.
It's a cold world they say,
yearning for a bon fire.
I used to hear it,
the beats of a warm heart,
but I fear that sound is extinct
because I've grown lonelier than an empty attic.
The terror of the fate of our future
roars like a fierce storm.
I'm scared
we may never see the light of day.

tick tock

Time is a powerful thing.
Too much of it can leave you bored.
 Not enough of it can drive you mad.
Any waste of it
is too dreadful to think.
What do you do with your time?

Time is a track star
because it sure moves fast!
You look up and say, dag, where did it go!

The answer to that, no one knows.
It is a tricky little something, time that is;
my, how it can laugh in your face.
One thing about time,
it demands respect,
because if you take it for granted,
it will put you in check.
What do you do with your time?

Time may move fast.
It may get cocky sometimes,
and it might not always
work in your favor.
But if there's one
thing I know about time,
it has no favorites.
Time knows no rules,
can and will be cruel,
and give you reasons to doubt.
But no matter how
fast time moves,
time does run out.

What do you do with your time?

Trapped

Inevitable,
are the problems
of this world.
Creditable,
everyone.
They say we evolved
from each other.

~ Blue Rose ~
Poetry Novel

We are necessary
for one another
to survive.
So is it fair to say
I'm the necessary
cause when you die?
Who am I?
but a human being -
Or am I a parasite
to everything you think?
The poisons we intoxicate:
death
hate.
The very
things that bring harm
are the very
things we own.
I am my own weapon
of mass destruction
built by human instructions.
Alive
from what I am fed:
a plate of left-over
self inflictions.
There is no cure
for the poisons I breathe
unless I
stop breathing
which would stop
my heart from beating,
so what is my ticket out?
Hate.
Survival of the fittest
until I'm fitted down.

Stand

idk is a deaf place that can leave you potentially alone. Standing on soil between knowledge and blurred vision, my future has not yet been mentioned, and I'm lost regarding decisions. Waiting, standing still, incomplete. What's to become of me? What will happen next? Good, bad, or ugly? The decision maker knows all, and has not yet revealed. I'm blind waiting for the fold to disappear from my eyelids. Time is on chill and I'm biting fingernails. I suppose I'll just chill too, and let time do its job. After all, when then becomes now, it'll be a mystery solved.

the sky roars

Rain pit pats my
window all night.
Light. Slow.
Heavy. Fast.
It goes thrash
crash against
the pane. Thunder
shakes the house.
Lightning strikes.
I wonder if
the car outside
will be alright.
Bed. Pillow.
Blanket. Ceiling.
Insomnia.

Verb

I wanted to hate you but I found no use. So I did the only thing I could do. I picked up a pen. The world is full of disappointment and it disappoints me to realize it won't stop disappointing.

I could wait for a change, but I'd be waiting forever. I hate broken promises and don't understand why they're made at all. A disappointing world creates broken hearts. My heart isn't in a million pieces. It's just been slightly torn. The fact that it's not whole, however, causes me to mourn, causes me to hate, causes me to push away, and eventually, causes me to write.

I write for my broken heart and the broken hearts of others. For those whose dreams caused them disappointment. My appointment was in satisfaction, happiness, sanity, pleasure; but now that's all been dissed. What to do now? How to feel now? Where to go now? Nowhere. Just sit in silence, continuing to dream about how it could've been.

I've experienced the past, now I'm trying to landscape my future. The world is made to disappoint, I just have to find the goodness in it. I've been let down, had my heart torn, been lied to, and somewhere in there I have to find a reason to smile. I know I will, eventually, but how long will that be is the question now.

I sit on a rock between pain and laughter. My hand rests on pain, but it hurts so badly now, I must move. Laughter, peace, and joy want me to join; and I want too. In given time, I'll take that step, but for now, I'll just be cool.

When I'm ready to move, I'll take paper and pen to make the ride smooth. To get from where I've been; I'll just write.

the tongue

Tell me what I can't do,
and I'll be determined to
prove you wrong.
If opposites attract
then we have the tightest bond.
They use my weakness
to bring me harm,
yet I use it to make
myself stronger.
Only fools speak
negative of me and
find themselves in
doubt. I speak
a mother load
without opening
my mouth. Those
who tell me I can't
are yet to be swept.
But what do I do
when I tell it to
myself?

Dysfunction

There used to be a time when it was
normal for children to bury parents but
now the cycle has reversed.
There used to be a time when I
could fall asleep and have bad dreams
but lately my nightmares haunt me
midday when I'm wide awake.
What is one to say?

I can't. I can not function. I can
not think. I can not sleep.
And I am fighting to breathe.
I'm alive but I am not here
because I can't find you.

I used to hate math. It
was too complicated.
Now I respect it
because it always provides
answers to every equation.
There are some things in life
I can't make sense of;
wish it were like
math and give me a
reason why.

Break it down.
Figure it out.
Crack it open.
It may take days but
the problem could always
be solved.
Death is not math at all.

Kamaya Thompson

Murder has no answer.
A bullet has no solvent.
I can understand some
depths of death like,
old age, disease, or
it was just their time.
But there is no
logical explanation for
entering a bullet into
the heart of a nine
month year old infant.

Where is the answer
to that? How can you
explain taking a
mother the age half of
forty-eight, gunning
her down without
remorse, only rage.
And please justify the
answer while looking
into the eyes of her
three year old child.

Such an equation can
only be solved by a genius.
It's a shame, only an idiot
could think it up.

Still, I believe
even for the greatest
mastermind it is too much.
Death is not math.
Murder can never be solved.

Senseless matter – why
should it exist at all?

title for my tears

They try to make me mad for simply feeling angry.
They want to knock me down, but that just ain't me.
I want to die some days, because I see no reason to
live but I continue to breathe, because it may get
better towards the end.

When I'm crying, I find a reason to laugh.
Yet they laugh when they see me crying.
Life is so unfair.
Sometimes, I want to knock her down and leave her
dead. But then I realize I'd only be hurting myself.
I'm at the point where I'm too old to stay, and too old
to run. Yet if I don't act at all it causes people to
wonder. I see every move before it happens, but bad
situations are what I fail to avoid. I'm not dumb, it's
just that my courage still holds a question mark. I
want to grow, but only with its given time. For if I
run ahead, my steps will be forced to rewind.

When I speak, I'm never heard, no matter how
clearly I pronounce each word. The world doesn't
always learn through verbs, so I'm better off writing
than letting my lips curl. No one will ever experience
my pain, but if they can just feel it, they'll be forced
to retain.

You may not know me, be able to see or hear me…
but we can be best friends if through art we can feel.

My purpose is to pass this on. The earth revolves through the work of the palm.

i hate love

she takes control of the tongue and ties it up or sometimes she loosens it and makes it slip – spitting words of embarrassment. she snaps the knees and makes them weak or may even stiffen them until the joints dare not move a peep. she puts insects in the stomach and spins the intestines around. she rolls the eyes and widens the lashes and drops the jaw and foams the lip and raises the brow; itches the scalp and stutters the sentence once rehearsed. she quenches the thirst. and it is exactly when you are face to face that she does you in. everybody knows her name, there's no need to explain, introduce, or make way; because she makes her own way into your head. she sneaks up on you and leaves a crave. her language resides in the eyes. her home dwells in your mind. and her intuition slips between your thighs. she is heavy-handed, when she hits it stings and triggers memories every time the act is repeated. she has a tight grip, beware of her visit. though she may exit, she leaves a scent. an annoying fragrance you can't forget and inevitably can't resist. it is difficult to determine when she may return. but each day, her knock at the door is what the body yearns. she is a bitch. the body is her whore. i never thought I'd be slave to a four letter word.

you are you are

If you're still awake, I hope my spirit taps your soul. Let this pen bring you knowledge that I will never let you go. Friend is a lousy title. You're my sister, bf, homie, shawty, - angel, if nothing else. We've been down for a couple of years, but it seems like we've been down forever.

So let it begin. Let it be forever. That's my intention anyhow. Real friends may travel apart but they still walk the same mile. I want you to know wherever you are, even when your soul is in the sky, that just because the situation might look dead, it doesn't mean I've died; for I can write. I'm writing for us, to keep us alive. I'm writing to let the world know you and I are bound for life.

If you need me, I'm here. If you want me, I'm closer than near. If you just want to chat, call or text. If you're feeling bad, my ears are leant. When you're down, consider my shoulder your pillow. Need some help, I'm your hero. Even when you make me mad or get on my last nerve, nothing in this world can come between our circle. You're my heart and I need you to breathe. You're the very living part of me.

Everything I am has been inspired by you. You're my best friend and that will never change. So wherever you are, if your pillow is wet, as I envision it is; know now, my spirit dries your tears. Know that when you cry, you don't cry alone, because you and I are one.

Kamaya Thompson

i am F'n sexy

I used to be scurred.
Used to be like, naw.
Now I'm all over
myself like four
corners on a wall.
Ain't it funny,
pressure and peers
and things. Haha
I laugh, 'cause it's
no longer bothering
me. Yesterday it
would hurt to say
I love myself,
but today it's as
common as Chris
and Rihanna drama.
I am so fly.
I walk pass the mirror
and don't wana say
goodbye. I am so
stuck on I,
like collar and tie.
There is nothing
blue about my looks.
It's obvious I look
good, and I feel
good too. As a matter
of fact, I'm like a bowl
of Frosted Flakes…
I'm more than good,
I'm grrreeeaaatttt!!!
Don't misperceive, this
is not conceit

but certainty.
I take pride in being
myself and that's
a far cry from the
place that I've been.
Yes, please, and
checkmate. I've
made an upgrade.
Damn, I'm hotter
than that thang.

minutes

new year's resolutions
are outdated. fear is
overrated. time is here,
tomorrow not guaranteed.
basically, my life has
no warranty. if you reply,
maybe our love will grow.
regarding the future, I'll
never know. I live for
today because it's all I can
do. what I know of, surely,
each minute I live it's
loving you. no need to fake,
I can't get you off my mind.
All I ask: that the clock
continue to turn hands 'til
your hand twines with mine.

Kamaya Thompson

Weirdo

will they see me or label
me what I am on the
outside will I be accepted
or rejected as an outsider
when will my reflection
show who I am inside will I
ever know who I am
entirely if life is only for
now will my life be vowed
or stricken down this is a
battle and I don't know
who wins but I don't think I
am the weird kid is weird
for a reason or is this
weirdness only here for a
season I don't know is the
hardest answer no doubt
but it's even harder coming
out what's this thing called
life all about

Ink

The universe is divinely created
to bring things together in such
a way that man cannot control.
Everything that happens has a
purpose; and that is a life's
goal. Success is found when
one understands that
experience is home to

knowledge. No one can control
their destiny despite how hard
they try. Life is a gift meant to
cherish in all its glory. Life
never ends, only does breath.
The spirit is an ongoing story.

Motivation

If tomorrow doesn't come
I want you to know
that for you I will go.
With arms open wide,
no looking back,
no strings attached,
I'll make it better
so you can see
that there is nothing
we can't achieve.
If you want to fly,
I'll be your wings.
I'll sacrifice all my
precious things
because you are more
precious to me.
I'll be the hero
so at the end of this
story no villain can
destroy what we've
built. We've built
a connection.
We've built a bond.
We share blood
and I vow to give honor.

Kamaya Thompson

For our name's sake
I'll carry the weight.
Your face gives me
strength.
Your voice
motivates me to
push on.
Your laughter
pumps my heart.
You are my wheel.
I am driven.
Kyla,
your name keeps me
living.

can't say it enough

three words
those three words;
so important,
yet I keep forgetting
to let them slip from my tongue

three words
just three little words
so simple,
yet their meaning is humungous,
they can change a life
and save a soul

so, just in case
I don't say it enough
I will learn to say it a lot
I don't know when

~ Blue Rose ~
Poetry Novel

I'll run out of time

even if you don't
say it in return
let me know if I
say it too much,
that way I'll know I've done it right

don't let life be in vain
speak those words
and know that you mean it

you never know
when you'll regret
not saying it
so say it
as much as you can

I love you!
tell every one you know

I love you!
change a life
save a soul

I love you!
pass it on
I love you!
and so on and so on….

I love you!

New Chapter

Set my cold heart on fire. Burn it until it's too hot to hold. Heat my frozen heart. Defrost it until all the icicles are gone. I know I've asked for redemption one too many times, but I need you or I'll go out of my mind. I'm not perfect, but I could be worst. I could not know you, and be without rebirth. So, dear God, hear my plea. Create a clean heart within me.

Trivial Love

Damn this stupid gift. Its beauty is only a myth disguised as powerful, able to change. It's not! Ignorance is only to blame. How dumb of me to think this pen could save the world. It's useless, can only allow eyes to read, but can mentally save no one. I thought I could save them. I thought I could bring them back. I thought I could let go of these fears attached to my heart, but I can't. Not with this pen. Not with this voice. Not with these hands. Not with these lips. My passion, desires, love, deepest thoughts can not keep the world safe from harm. Can not heal the ill. Can not eject a bullet from one's wound. Can not erase the horrid images from a victim's crown. I am only human. Only my parents' child. I can not save the world. And I doubt anyone can save me.

I Don't Care

real love
doesn't give a @#$%!

~ Blue Rose ~
Poetry Novel

---

real love
does not judge
real love
is secure
real love
is pure
real love
doesn't care who you are or where you've been
real love
is complete
real love
is not weak
real love
does not pick and choose
real love
says do what you do
real love
does not complain
real love
has no restraints
real love
holds tight and never lets go
real love
never loses a battle
real love
heals
real love
dries tears
real love
does not reside on a two way street
real love
is deep
real love
caresses
real love

forgives
real love
admits truth and hates lying
real love
will never leave you alone
real love
is a place you can call home
real love
isn't many things, but it is true
I'm glad I found real love in you
And for the record,
I really love you too

Anonymous

7 years behind.
Thought I was 7 years ahead.
Can't believe she said I
act like I'm 12.
Everything I've worked hard
for falls harder
than the raindrops on my
window pane.
My identity is a thunderstorm
again. My emotions are worn
like the tee on my back. I
can't hide who I am
and simultaneously can't deny
myself as well.
I can't deny my anonymity.
The frustration boils hotter
than the tea I sip. Not even
chamomile can bring
genuine tranquility. I have

become disgusted with this baby
face. These dimples on my cheeks.
These wide eyes set me behind. Why
must youth reside? My maturity is
constantly slapped with I-M.
I am so lost. I am so lost. I am?

arms open

If utopia exists then this must be it.
I'm just happy today.
I'm scared actually.
I've never felt this way.
I appreciate life.
I'm free.
My heart is skipping beats.
My smile is sincere.
I've never felt sheer, genuine
peace, love, and respect.
Life is a gift.
My heart is flooded.
It's a beautiful day.
I'm happy and can't explain why.
And that absent reason makes life
even brighter.

Divine Order

And I thought my corner was bare.
Apparently my shoulder isn't so heavy.
I now have a shoulder to rest my head.
Fear is escaping me.
I clearly see alone isn't quite my zone.

I can make this house a home –
And I wanted to be left alone;
boy was I wrong.
Hearts beat beyond the pace I
thought they'd skip. I was trippin'.
Love is unconditional and can last forever.
One word I won't ever say is never.

happy birthday!

mental capacity
at large. can't fit anymore
bullshit
inside.
that's what's become
of my life.
the people pleaser
of the world sacrifices your
expectations for
desires of her own. and
I don't feel bad about it
at all.
thank you very much.

home alone

Life sucks when it's cold outside and the world is quiet and getting gifts day is just around the corner. Lying in bed, staring at the ceiling, pc on my chest equals no entertainment when surfing has turned into boredom. I'd procrastinate if I could, but this time I have no task to make procrastination a task. Conversations are too much a deed. All I can process is think, breathe, and eat. The sky grows darker, the numbers on the clock increase. A day is gone. As has my energy.

if only

If only we could see the future
would it make us rethink our present.
It is only when the future becomes
our present that we regret our past.
If only I knew then what I know now,
is a statement I've heard far too often
in this life. If only. If only. If only
too late meant we had more time.

marionette

Insomnia grants Tom and Jerry at 6am
and as my eyes dare to shut, my mind
scorns with refusal. To construct the mind
with homework assignments is a thought
ignored. Rainy streets and muddy grass
keep my feet cuddled in this warm fleece.
My body wants to move, muscles refuse.
Only metacarpal limbs have the upper
hand…The exact reason I am writing this.

Premonition

Nothing surprises me anymore.
I will not be so naïve to believe
that life follows rules or even
cares about one's ambitions. Life
is spontaneous, free-willed, and
quite selfish at times.

I awoke to a window of flooded
snow as the first day of spring
arrived one week ago. If flakes
can atop budded trees and a nine
month infant can take her last
breath before me, then I am
subject to die today.

Jonathan Larson's notes go
ringing in my head. No day but
today exhales then inhales back
again. Although I hold
Mr. Bubbles tight through the
night, I still manage to arise
before the alarm fulfills its
purpose.

I am sleep deprived by my
purpose. Debating and negotiating
summer and fall in spring;
coordinating change in an
unchanged season. I bleed my
ink, tongue, and throat in your
name because tomorrow is not a
promised date. So I promise to
uplift your names today.

Foresight and foreshadow.
Sankofa. A tattoo on brown skin.
NovAva, my respiratory quench.

what pain feels like

It feels like rubber tugging away
at my throat. Liquid pupils, tranquil
pulse. Extended digits as the center
of the palm resists forming fists.
I am fighting death.

Pushing beyond a universal force
that laughs in my face all the reasons
I have not to rejoice. I swallow tears.
Nerves bulging from my brain.
Ponytails getting looser by the day.
Ignoring my wrists when I shave.
Today is not that day.

The ignorance as to when that
day will occur drives me to
push a little further.
I've something to live for.
What are you?
Why are you testing me?

Weeks announce a celebration
of 19 years of life, yet I refuse to X
the calendar because time is a lousy
son of a bitch and I refuse to pay him
any attention. Time steals.
Time cheats. Time destroys families.

And time is no physician certified to
heal all wounds. Time makes
the smartest man a fool and does it so
cleverly it receives praises in the end.
Time is no one's fucking friend.
Only a gotdamn hypocrite.
So why am I here?

Is life only a passing road to death?
And if so, am I only wasting time
by not ending it myself?
Suicide is equivalent to *ask the audience*.

I am starving. I am stuffed.
I am joyful. I feel like I've been hit by a bus.
I am sprinting. I am learning to crawl.
I am growing, only to feel small.
I am healthy. I am diseased.
I am confident. I've low self esteem.
I am whole. I am chaffing away.
I am companied. I'm lonelier than a dried lake.
I am secure. I am shallow.
I am smiling. But not on the inside.
I am dying with the breath of life.

To You

Hey you,
who didn't get the chance to live a year.
And you, whose heart stopped
before we could meet again.
And you too, mother,
who never got to see her
daughter take her first steps.

~ Blue Rose ~
Poetry Novel

And the rest of you, with
bodies of breath.
I will do my best.
I shall give my all.
Sign your name across my
heart. No way is it over yet.
It has only just begun.
For I'm thinking of
what Sarah said. That,
love is watching someone die.
And I can't sleep at night
without crying.
This is all I have.
With this pen and heart,
I promise.

www.ingramcontent.com/pod-product-compliance
Lightning Source LLC
Chambersburg PA
CBHW031258290426
44109CB00012B/641